Bentwood

TANYA BARTER

JOHN DUNNIGAN

SETH STEM

MUSEUM OF ART

RHODE ISLAND SCHOOL OF DESIGN

1984

EXHIBITION DATES

Part I:
A History of Bentwood
January 13 – April 29, 1984

Part II:
Bentwood Today
March 16 – April 29, 1984

This project has been supported by a grant
from the National Endowment for the Arts, a
Federal agency.

Design: Gilbert Associates
Printing: Eastern Press

Table of Contents

Lenders to the Exhibition

Anonymous lenders
Bancroft Sporting Goods Company, Woonsocket, Rhode Island
George Considine
Timothy Curtis
Peter Danko
John Dunnigan
William Hammersley
Harwood Gallery, New York, New York
Maryjane Heyman
Thomas Hucker
Lawrence B. Hunter
Dakota Jackson
The Manney Collection
Alphonse Mattia
The Metropolitan Museum of Art, New York, New York
Museum of Art, Rhode Island School of Design
Museum of Fine Arts, Boston, Massachusetts
The Museum of Modern Art, New York, New York
Mystic Seaport Museum, Mystic, Connecticut
Old Sturbridge Village, Sturbridge, Massachusetts
Jere Osgood
Martha Rising
Roitman & Son, Inc., Providence, Rhode Island
Society for the Preservation of New England Antiquities,
    Boston, Massachusetts
Seth Stem
Mrs. Bernard Weinstein
Richard Wickstrom
William A. Farnsworth Library and Art Museum, Rockland, Maine
Wunsch Americana Foundation, New York, New York

Foreword

The Rhode Island School of Design has had a long involvement with furniture design based upon the woodworking techniques of bending and lamination. Mrs. Gustav Radeke, President of the School from 1913 to 1931 and also head of the Museum, was an early collector of Windsor chairs. An 1888 photograph of her husband, Dr. Radeke, shows him seated in a large comb-back Windsor from their collection. Wallace Nutting, the chronicler of early American furniture and interiors, also recognized Mrs. Radeke's pioneering role in collecting Windsors, and in his book *A Windsor Handbook* (published in 1917), he illustrates several examples from her collection.

As in other areas of art, Mrs. Radeke used her eye and collection to benefit the Museum of which she was in charge. Of the large collection of Windsor chairs in the Museum virtually all derive from a Radeke source. Beginning in 1918 Windsors were accessioned as gifts from Mrs. Radeke, or were bought for the collection under her direction. A bill dated 1920 from Wallace Nutting survives for one of the Museum's writing-arm Windsors. The bill is interesting not only as documentation of the object, but also as a record of the close association Mrs. Radeke had with Nutting. In 1931 the major portion of Mrs. Radeke's collection of early American furniture came to the Museum by bequest, and it is through this gift that the Windsor chair collection achieved its breadth from children's Windsors to continuous-arm Windsors.

As the twentieth century progressed, the Museum also took an interest in new developments in bentwood and lamination. In the 1930's an Alvar Aalto chair entered the collection, followed in the 1970's with examples by Josef Hoffmann and Charles Eames.

An 1888 photograph of Dr. Gustav Radeke seated in a comb-back Windsor chair

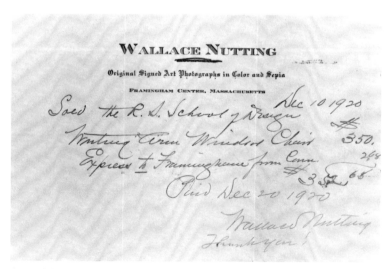

A 1920 bill from Wallace Nutting for a writing-arm Windsor chair

In more recent years the Museum has actively sought to fill significant gaps in this historical collection, as well as to keep abreast of current developments. As a result the Museum's bentwood collection has become an excellent design and teaching resource for these woodworking techniques.

The exhibition is a collaborative effort by several individuals who had an interest in different aspects of these two fascinating woodworking techniques. The historical section of the exhibition is based on John Dunnigan's research into the history of bentwood. The wonderful memory of Christopher Monkhouse, Curator of Decorative Arts at the Museum, has enabled us to assemble a fascinating group of objects to illustrate this history. Seth Stem, instructor in the woodworking department at RISD, has curated the contemporary portion of the exhibition in the course of which he has brought together the work of fourteen artists currently using bentwood and lamination. We hope the result is an exhibition which illustrates method, technique, and design in a manner which is both enjoyable and instructive for the casual visitor, scholar, artist and craftsman.

To produce an exhibition one must rely on the help of many. I wish to thank the respective staffs of both the Museum and the Office of Public Affairs who have been especially helpful and supportive. Finally, without the cooperation of the fourteen contemporary artists represented in the exhibition, the catalogue would not have materialized. To the above individuals, to the lenders, and to the National Endowment for the Arts, I wish to say thank you.

Tanya Barter
Assistant Curator of Decorative Arts

Bentwood chairs which antedate Michael Thonet's, left to right: American Windsor armchair, 18th century (RISD, Gift of the Estate of Mrs. Gustav Radeke 31.427); Samuel Gragg, Boston, Massachusetts, (1772–1855), "Elastic chair," ca. 1810 (Lent by the Wunsch Americana Foundation); Claude Chapuis, French, (active 1797–1818), armchair, ca. 1810 (RISD, Abby Rockefeller Mauzé Fund 81.200.1)

8

A History of Bentwood

For more than two thousand years artists have repeatedly tried to recapture the ideal of perfection found in ancient Greek art. No less canonical than the statue of the Spear Bearer by Polykleitos or the Parthenon itself, the Greek klismos (chair) has been an inspiration for furniture designers from the Romans to Thomas Hope to Tage Frid. The klismos has been considered by many to be an ideal in furniture. It stands on four curved legs that gracefully support the body and it has a backrest that cradles the upper body. Although it is not known exactly how these curved chair parts were made originally, craftsmen since have tried many different methods to reinterpret the form.

Two of the better known figures of late eighteenth and early nineteenth century Neo-Classicism, Robert Adam and Thomas Hope, designed chairs and other furniture with sweeping curves that must have challenged contemporary veneering technology. Their requirements alone did not cause a dramatic change in the state of the art, but it is more than coincidence that by the 1820's new machinery had been invented to saw veneer in great quantity. What had once been done through a very painstaking process was now easily produced by a steam-powered machine. With this in mind, it is interesting to consider the various Classical Revival styles from the point of view of curves and veneer.

Generally speaking, there has existed throughout history a symbiotic relationship between style and technology which has manifested itself not only in the world of art and design, but also in utilitarian objects such as the barrel and the bow. Often the task at hand necessitated the development of new technology which in turn led to some other change or discovery. For example, it is difficult to imagine the development of civilization without the chariot wheel, bow and arrow, the sailing ship, or the Baroque violin. Sometimes fashion necessitates the technique and sometimes technology determines the style, but most often it is a little of each. The history of wood bending is an example of this phenomenon.

Of the many ways to obtain a curved piece of wood, there are several common to the objects brought together in this exhibition of bentwood and lamination. First, it is possible to utilize a naturally crooked root, trunk, or branch that approximates the desired shape and then to saw out the exact curve along the grain. This method has been used for many centuries in the construction of wooden boats and is still in use today by some traditional boatbuilders. Tamarack, a type of larch, produces fine natural crooks that are much sought after by shipwrights for use as stems. It is possible that furniture from antiquity such as the Greek klismos was made in this way. Before the demands of high production/high profit wood harvesting common in the twentieth century made this seem inefficient, a craftsman was able to obtain naturally curved pieces of wood.

Greek red-figured vase depicting a klismos chair, Attic, 5th century B.C. (RISD, gift of Charles Bradley and Museum Appropriation 22.114)

9

Perhaps the oldest method of bending wood is to take thin pieces of freshly cut, unseasoned wood and bend them into curves. The combination of small dimension and high moisture content allows many species of wood to be bent cold into even a very small radius. As long as the strips are restrained, they will keep their shape as the wood dries and loses its natural pliability. Baskets are often made in this way with the strips actually woven together to restrain them. Snowshoes are another example of a utilitarian object made by cold bending; the strips are often tied together at the ends to prevent them from straightening out.

The back of a Windsor chair, while usually not too much bigger in dimension than a snowshoe, cannot be as satisfactorily made by cold bending. To avoid unsightly surface cracks which appear when an unseasoned piece of wood dries, and to prevent unnecessary stress on the joinery, the wood is first seasoned and then steam-bent. A species of wood with a straight and long, porous grain structure such as hickory or ash is carefully seasoned until it reaches a moisture content of about twenty percent. It is milled to size, removing the surface checks or cracks that have appeared, and then made pliable by being subjected to boiling water or steam. The softened wood is clamped to a form of the desired shape and when it has cooled and dried, will more or less retain that shape. This too is an ancient technique used to make wheels for carriages and planking for ships, as well as for furniture.

Finally there is lamination. It is the process of gluing together several very thin strips or laminates into one curved piece. Once the glue has dried, it holds the laminates permanently in the desired shape. While the technique of gluing together thin veneers was known to the Egyptians by 1350 B.C. at the latest, laminating as a practical means of producing curved shapes in wood has gone in and out of favor many times since. There is perhaps no better

John Henry Belter, German (1804–1863), side chairs, ca. 1863, laminated rosewood (RISD, Given in memory of Mary Chew Miller and Commander William Davis Miller 77.087)

Michael Thonet, German (1796–1871), Boppard armchair, 1836–1840 (Gebrüder Thonet)

example of this than the work of John Henry Belter, who was born in Germany in 1804 and trained as a craftsman in the Biedermeier tradition before he emigrated to New York around 1840. He became famous for his Rococo Revival furniture which was constructed in an ingenious way. The shapes were made by laminating several sheets of rosewood veneer into a curved form and then sawing away parts and gluing on others before finally carving elaborate floral decorations into and onto them. The layers of veneer were glued so that each layer had its grain direction running perpendicular to the one adjacent which was in effect exceptionally stable like plywood. However, when Belter died in 1863, the limitations of the available glue and therefore of the entire method were already becoming apparent, and within ten years this type of laminated furniture had fallen into relative obscurity. Not until synthetic glues were developed for war technology (especially airplanes) during the first fifty years of this century, did lamination again become practical as a furniture-making technique. It is now considered to be the most efficient method of obtaining curved parts for a wide range of applications including architecture and furniture.

For a look at the development of wood bending during the last one hundred and fifty years and for some insight into how this technology came to affect the lives of many in a new way, it is worthwhile in particular to examine the life and work of Michael Thonet.

Long before the tenets of Modernism were accepted, in Michael Thonet's furniture form and function were one. Twentieth-century designers such as Breuer, Aalto, and Eames, as well as many contemporary designer-craftsmen, have been inspired by Thonet's bentwood techniques and timeless designs.

Michael Thonet (pronounced like sonnet and with a silent h) was born the son of a tanner in Boppard-am-Rhein, Germany, in 1796. He was apprenticed to a cabinetmaker, and by age 23 opened his own shop. By 1830 he was building furniture in the Biedermeier style, sometimes seen as a provincial version of the Paris *meubles de luxe*. Like Empire in France, Regency in England, and Federal in America, Biedermeier was fashionable in the first half of the nineteenth century.

Before long Thonet had established a reputation for technically skillful, innovative execution of traditional work. His earliest known bent work is in applied decorative elements on otherwise typical Biedermeier pieces. An engraving in the Technisches Museum in Vienna shows a set of furniture made between 1830 and 1840, illustrating an appliqué on the sofa and bed which is probably typical of the kind of work Thonet produced a decade earlier as well.

With the exception of the front and back seat rails and the back support, his chairs of this period are made entirely of laminated strips of veneer. The lamination was done by loosely tying a stack of veneer strips, each measuring about 1/16 inch by 1 inch by 84 inches, into a bundle and soaking it in a bath of hot glue. The glue was made from animal hide and bone. Once the bundle of veneer was completely saturated, it was removed from the bath and, before the glue started to set, pressed into a heated mold of the desired shape. After it was satisfactorily fastened to the form, the whole was left to cool and harden in place. After a couple of hours, Thonet had a curved piece of wood that was cheaper to make, lighter, and more durable than anything he could have carved out of solid wood. In addition, the inner laminations could be cut from less expensive wood than the outside surfaces.

Over the years Thonet tried several techniques in an attempt to perfect his laminating process. Not satisfied with the one-plane bends of the earlier Boppard chairs, he tried resawing an already laminated curve perpendicular to the glue lines and regluing it on a second curved plane. This process was slow and impractical; the reapplication of hot glue weakened the first set of glue joints, and there was also the problem of trying to bend all the hard glue in the first lamination. The resulting pieces were too costly to be marketed widely.

As a next experiment, Thonet cut thin rods of square cross section and tied them into a bundle. Sixteen rods ¼ inch by ¼ inch made a 1 inch by 1 inch part. The bundle was cooked in a hot glue bath and bent to a mold, as in the first process. Although these strips bent easily, it was difficult to achieve a uniform glue line, so this approach was also impractical.

Thonet kept returning to his original method using a single stack of flat laminates and eventually found that simply by twisting it he could obtain the compound curves he wanted. Rectilinear surfaces, when twisted, lie in different planes and thus a wood-strip laminate can be bent easily in more than one direction, depending on the amount of twist. It was the logical next step, but it took twenty years to figure out.

Thonet applied this new technique while working with the architect P. H. Desvignes on the Palais Liechtenstein. He designed three chairs, apparently the first of their kind, each composed of six bundles of laminates. The first bundle goes up one rear leg, forms part of the back, and continues down the other leg; another bundle forms the seat frame and part of the back; the legs and seat rails are made from a series of laminates going up one leg, across to support a section of the seat, and down the other leg. Each leg is thus made up of two bundles glued in turn to one another with triangular inserts in the corners. Entirely laminated, these chairs seem to be without mechanical joints or fasteners.

The Liechtenstein chairs reflect various furniture styles from about 1650 on. Their lines build upon the Louis XIV and Queen Anne styles of the late seventeenth and early eighteenth centuries and were influenced by the Rococo as well – in fact they were made to be used in a Rococo Revival setting in the palace. The Classical Revival was also a major ingredient – archaeological discoveries after 1750 brought ancient Egyptian, Greek, and Roman furniture to the eyes of a fashion-conscious public. The Greek klismos chair particularly attracted the attention of furniture makers, whose attempts to copy its graceful

Michael Thonet, German (1796–1871), Liechtenstein chair, 1843–1846 (The Royal Prince of Liechtenstein)

leg curves proved problematic: shaping from solid wood necessitated choosing grain configurations with too much distortion for large-scale production; techniques like bending and laminating were solutions. Products of early industrial technology as much as of an older desire to imitate the art of the past, Thonet's Liechtenstein chairs constitute a crucial bridge between eighteenth and twentieth-century furniture.

Thonet developed another new chair in 1850. This one, for the Palais Schwarzenburg, had lathe-turned front legs doweled into the seat frame; the rear legs and backrest were laminated as in the Liechtenstein chairs. Certain changes in the process, however, make these chairs an important step toward solid bentwood furniture. Instead of a dozen or so thin layers of veneer cooked in glue, the backs use only four thicknesses of $5/16$ inch mahogany; the seat rings have five layers. Thonet cooked the laminates in boiling water, bent them on the forms and dried them for a few days, then glued them together; this required fewer laminates, which saved time, and the glue was under much less stress. This is the first chair Thonet constructed using the boiling-water technique, and it eventually appears as chair #1 in the Gebrüder Thonet catalogue.

In 1850 the family turned its attention to preparing for the great world exposition to be held the following year at the Crystal Palace in London. Thonet exhibited several pieces of furniture there, including a set of rosewood chairs and a settee with caned seats and backs in the Liechtenstein style. He sent pieces in mahogany and palisander as well, and tables with inlays of brass and tortoise shell. Thonet came away with a bronze medal (the highest awarded to an industrial product) and many important marketing contacts.

About this time Thonet received his first major public commission from the famous Café Daum in Vienna. From this point on, the bentwood chair would be known by many as the Café Chair. The back is made of four layers of twisted mahogany laminates, while the front legs appear to be bent from solid stock with turned capitals, which act as shoulders for the tenon of the leg into the seat. The seat frames are made of five layers of mahogany, as they were in the Schwarzenburg chairs. Because of its lightness, durability, and accommodating design, the bentwood chair was perfectly suited for public places. According to Hermann Heller, Thonet's biographer, Thonet shortly thereafter did a similar set of four hundred chairs for a hotel in Budapest.

Over the next three years Thonet, then almost 60, began to realize his lifelong goal of mass-producing solid bentwood chairs. He had been experimenting all along with solid-wood bending and had earlier tried with little success to bend slats for chair parts by cooking them in hot glue. It worked with the veneer but not with thicker stock. Having perfected the laminating process in the 1840's, Thonet continued to use thicker and fewer laminations in each successive design and with every passing year. In the mid-1850's he made another chair for the Palais Schwarzenburg which had a solid bentwood back made of one continuous rod that was full thickness in the rear legs but tapered to a thin strip at the top of the back where the bend was most critical. After it

Michael Thonet, German (1796–1871), Café Daum chair, ca. 1850 (Gebrüder Thonet)

was bent, two additional thin strips were laminated to this top section to regain the desired thickness. The seat frame was made up of only three layers, which probably were also boiled, bent, and dried before being glued.

The success of these products – not only Thonet's chairs but all kinds of furniture – was remarkable. The impetus gained from the Crystal Palace exhibition propelled the company into a worldwide market, and this, perhaps more than any other factor, conditioned the final form of the solid bentwood chair. Thonet had successfully shipped laminated chairs to several countries, but when he sent his first shipments to North and South America, he found that the glue would not stand up to prolonged heat and excessive moisture. Although Thonet had been working diligently to solve such problems for most of his life, it is no small coincidence that the fate of the solid, steam-bent chair was resolved at the moment when the vast American market was to be gained or lost.

The problem with bending solid wood of substantial thickness was that it always broke first on the convex surface, regardless of how much boiling water or steam it was subjected to. The fibers stretched and tore apart on this outside face, while their compression on the inside or concave surface usually caused no damage. The very center of the piece probably remained constant in length and therefore neutral. To solve the problem, Thonet needed a way to keep the convex side of the bend from stretching, to make it act more like the neutral layer, and to transform the force of the bend entirely into compression. He fastened a strip of sheet iron to a still-straight piece of wood on what would be the convex surface and squeezed it at the ends with screw clamps. When the piece was bent, the convex side of the curve could not stretch, and the whole piece was under uniform compression – as though the neutral layer of fibers had been moved to the outer edge of the wood. Bending in more than one direction simply required additional straps.

To apply this technique to his furniture, Thonet first had to find a suitable wood. Mahogany, rosewood, and palisander, which laminated well, did not bend in solid rods as easily as ash or beech. The long, straight grain of beech, coupled with its low cost, made it the logical choice. The process followed these lines: a straight-grained, branchless beech butt was crosscut to the desired length in the forest to avoid hauling unnecessary wood back to the shop. The log was ripsawn into rods of square section (approximately 2′ x 2′) and then turned to the desired shape on a lathe. Next, a rod was selected, probably before drying, and steamed for one to two hours, depending on its thickness. When the rod was pliable enough, it was quickly placed in the iron strap (or straps) and bent by hand on a cast-iron form to the desired shape. This could take only a couple of minutes. After the wood and strap were clamped to the form, the whole thing was placed in a heated room for a few days to dry. By this method Thonet could make the rear legs and back of a chair out of one long piece of solid wood, eliminating much of the joinery chairs previously required and avoiding the short grain weakness of sawn or carved joints. The front legs and seat rims went through an identical process on their way from log to chair. The legs were turned and tapered before they

Detail of tearing on the convex surface in course of bending wood

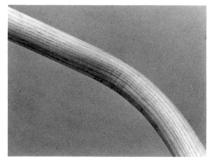

Detail of collapse on the concave surface in course of bending wood

were bent, but the seats were bent, glued, and screwed with a scarf joint and then finally the edges were rounded.

Thonet built his first factory at Koritshan in Moravia (now Czechoslovakia) in 1856; he designed not only the factory but much of its machinery (multi-bladed saws to mill the stock and a mechanical spoke-shaver to round and taper the rods) as well. The factory was situated at the edge of a beech forest, and it was powered completely by water and steam.

Thonet's factory made the transition from the artisan's small workshop to mass production, and by 1859 the technique of bending solid wood into almost any shape had been perfected. In that year Thonet designed his most popular chair, the #14 side chair, which retains the fluid lines of the Liechtenstein chairs while reinterpreting them as mass-produced items. Thonet reduced the chair to a minimum of six parts, easily produced, shipped, and assembled, since the members were bolted or screwed together. The front legs no longer had capitals at the joints, and they were screwed into the seat with threaded mortise and tenons. The chair cost less than the average worker earned in a week, and it became the company's best seller – fifty million sold in the first fifty years. Here was a chair elegant enough for the finest salons and inexpensive enough for the masses.

John Dunnigan
Part-time Faculty
Interior Architecture

Gebrüder Thonet, German (founded 1853), #18 sidechair or "Export Chair," 1876 (Gebrüder Thonet)
A variation on the 1859 #14 sidechair, the #18 sidechair proved to be especially popular in America.

Michael Thonet, German (1796–1871), Boppard chair, 1836–1840 (Gebrüder Thonet)

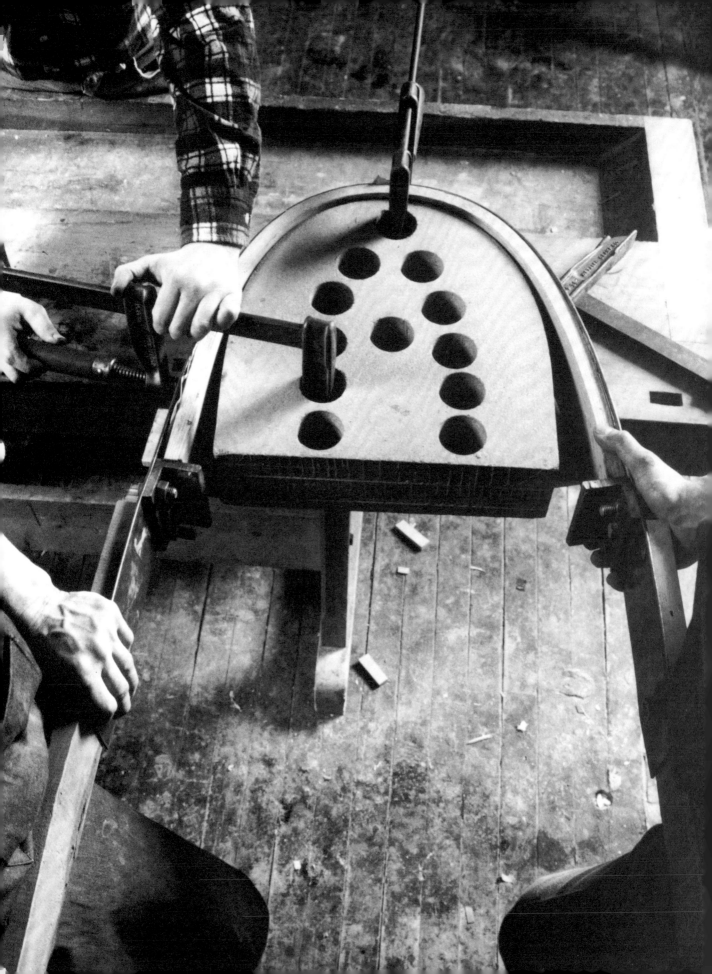

Bentwood Today

Wood has the natural propensity to attract attention because of its warmth, richness, and unique surface patterns and textures of unending variety. An almost mysterious property of wood is its ability to bend, in some cases having flexibility and memory to return to its original form, and in others to retain a predetermined curved shape. It is this bending property and its infinite variety of applications that we wish to illustrate in this exhibition of bentwood objects.

Furniture makers have historically dealt with bentwood to obtain curved form and structural strength in their designs. With the exception of Michael Thonet's bentwood furniture, I do not believe there has been a time period in history when bentwood has been used with such impact and flamboyance as in the last fifteen years. Modern technology has aided freedom of expression and design options to some extent, especially in the area of adhesives used in lamination work, but the foremost reason new work has come about is due to the renewed interest in woodworking and furniture as works of art.

During the 1970's a great deal of work with a high visual impact appeared because furniture makers treated furniture as an art form rather than as a purely functional object. Steam and laminate bending became a process vehicle for producing dynamic forms in wood. Much of the new creativity and exploration occurred on the West Coast in work by furniture makers and sculptors who, in the absence of a woodworking tradition there, had a fresh approach to dealing with the material involved. This new attitude carried over to the East Coast work, and technical information and artistic approaches were synthesized. A crossover between sculpture and furniture developed, of which bentwood was an important part.

Wood can be formed into simple curves (those bending in one plane) or compound curves (those bending in two planes simultaneously). Some of the processes used to produce both types of curves were expanded from instrument-making techniques, notably by Michael Jean Cooper and Robert Strini in California. Work in this exhibition illustrates the three most common woodbending techniques used: steam-bending, laminate bending, and bent plywood. For the practical furniture maker and the furniture industry, bentwood can offer the advantages of strength (wood fibers follow the curved form, thus avoiding weak points), can eliminate joinery, and can reduce the making of a furniture object to virtually a one-step process. In other cases, introducing curves in a design can greatly complicate the making of a piece, because square references are lost, and most woodworking machinery is set up to deal with straight lines and surfaces. Form work and bending jigs can become quite complex, requiring far more time to design and construct than would be required in actually bending the wood itself.

An overview of the varied approaches in utilizing the bentwood process is evident in the exhibition, from production-oriented design to the subtle curves of the more traditional furniture maker to the flamboyance and visual excitement exhibited in work by sculptors and furniture artists. These expressions will hopefully lead us to view furniture objects in a new perspective, showing us that a strong visual function can exist for these objects as well as a utilitarian one. There is no bentwood "style" that has come out of this period. The work is as varied and diverse as the traditions and backgrounds of the people who make it.

Seth Stem
Instructor
Industrial Design

The Catalogue

BRUCE BEEKEN

MICHAEL JEAN COOPER

TIMOTHY P. CURTIS

PETER J. DANKO

JOHN DUNNIGAN

WILLIAM S. HAMMERSLEY

THOMAS HUCKER

LAWRENCE B. HUNTER

DAKOTA JACKSON

WILLIAM KEYSER

ALPHONSE MATTIA

JERE OSGOOD

MARTHA LYNN RISING

SETH LAWRENCE STEM

Bruce Beeken

Shelburne, Vermont

Born 1953

Educated at Boston University (Certificate of
Mastery 1978), under Simon Watts, Putney,
Vermont (1973–74), under Carl Bausch,
Charlotte, Vermont (1972)

Selected Exhibitions: *A Case for Boxes*,
Museum of Art, Rhode Island School of Design,
1980; *Bruce Beeken/Furniture*, Vermont State
Craft Center at Frog Hollow, Middlebury,
Vermont, 1980; *New Handmade Furniture*,
Museum of Contemporary Crafts, New York,
1979; *Young Americans*, Museum of
Contemporary Crafts, New York, 1977–79

Artist's Statement:

The tea cart comes from the simple lines of some tools and vehicles of the
nineteenth century. It is derived from the undecorated forms of farm tools
made of steam-bent and shaped parts. The lyrical scythe and hayfork and a
nicely shaped plowshare achieve a balance between aesthetic and functional
considerations.

The tea cart also borrows from the lightness and fluent form of early high-
wheeled bicycles and is akin to the expression of motion and rhythm that
carriage makers lent to their craft.

Tea cart. Bruce Beeken. 1981. White ash. 32⅜″ x 21¾″ x 42″ (Museum of Art, Rhode Island
School of Design, Dr. Herbert H. Myers and Mary B. Jackson Funds 81.298)

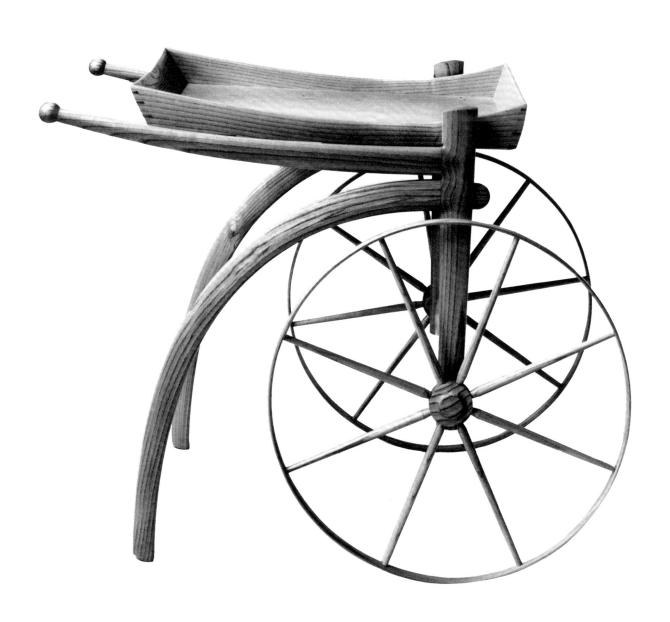

Michael Jean Cooper

Sebastopol, California

Born 1943

Educated at the University of California, Berkeley (MFA 1969), San Jose State College (MA 1968, BFA 1966)

Selected Exhibitions: *Annual Exhibition*, American Academy in Rome, Rome, 1980; *Royal Show*, Melbourne, Australia, 1979; *SECA Award 1977*, San Francisco Museum of Modern Art, 1977; *American Crafts 76*, Museum of Contemporary Art, Chicago, 1976

Artist's Statement:

There is a special joy that one experiences when ideas begin to develop and dovetail with the constructed objects. For me, the *process* is the major key. First come the thoughts, then maybe some sketches, lots more thinking, and finally a start, usually at an important area that is fairly clear in my mind. This then becomes a *reality* that serves to develop and clear up the foggy areas of the "non-piece." Finally, I feel that the process becomes a lifestyle. It becomes part of you and begins to stretch and push your own personal boundaries as it takes its own shape.

Soapbox racer. Michael Jean Cooper. 1976. Laminated red oak, aluminum, rubber, steel, nylon, plexiglas. 28″ x 50″ x 144″ (Richard Wickstrom Collection)

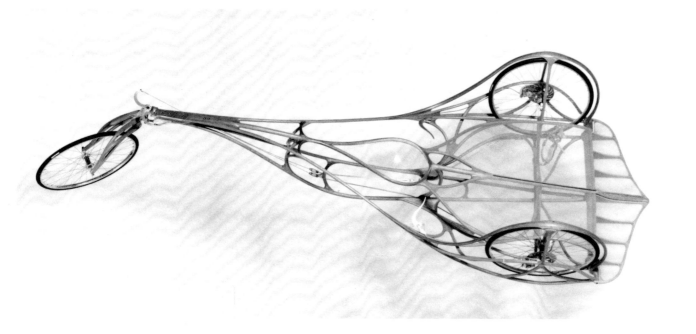

Timothy P. Curtis

St. Louis, Missouri

Born 1947

Educated at the University of California,
Berkeley (MFA 1979), San Diego State
University, California (MA 1978, BFA 1974)

Selected Exhibitions: *National Wood
Invitational*, Craft Alliance, St. Louis,
Missouri, 1983; *First Annual Midwest
Furniture Show and Competition*, Hibdon
Hardwood, St. Louis, Missouri, 1983; *Public
Sculpture for the 80's*, St. Louis, Missouri,
1983; *1981 Annual National Exhibition*, Texas
Fine Arts Association, Austin, Texas, 1981

Artist's Statement:

Browsing about one day I saw a croquet set in a display window. I immediately wrote a check for $30 and went home to play croquet. It was not as I had remembered from my childhood; playing croquet as a kid is much more fun. Playing games is an integral part of growing up and being a child can be a very surrealistic experience. As I recall, the mallets were very heavy and much too large to handle, the balls were giant and there must have been a hundred wire hoops to trip over . . . and don't spill the grownups' drinks. Generally, the rules were made as you went along.

As an adult, croquet is extremely detailed and ritualistic. It consists of six balls, six mallets, nine wickets, and two goal posts, all of which are ordinarily stored on a cart. The wickets are put in the ground according to a specific layout and the goal posts indicate the start and finish of the game. The mallets and balls are color coded to help maintain the order of play. While playing adult croquet many childhood experiences came to mind. Everything was big then, bikes with trainer wheels, toys too big to handle, and you had to grow into your baseball glove. Way back then it was normal to run, jump, and wrestle with each other in the grass. Nowadays things don't seem so big, many things are cheap and tacky, and no one has the time to play games. Touching each other can be socially uncomfortable and grass is meant to be smoked. I decided to put the fun back into adult croquet; my set was "gonna" be neat.

In order to recapture the surrealistic quality and spirit of childhood, I felt it was essential to construct the set on an enlarged scale. To stimulate viewer interaction, I built the mallets to react to the human form. In this way it becomes necessary that the players explore and discover each mallet to understand how it functions.

Croquet set. Timothy P. Curtis. 1977–78. Hardwood. 5' x 4' x 6' (Curtis Collection)

Peter J. Danko

Alexandria, Virginia

Born 1949

Educated at the University of Maryland
(BA 1971)

Selected Exhibitions: *Innovative Furniture in
America: 1800 to Present,* Cooper-Hewitt
Museum, New York, 1980; *New Handmade
Furniture,* American Crafts Museum, New
York, 1979

Artist's Statement:

My years as a craftsman have given me a strong respect for, and an intimate knowledge of, the qualities of wood and other materials. In my furniture, I try to relate this knowledge with all elements being necessary or complementing what is necessary. My designs reflect, in their functionalism, the forms and shapes I find beautiful in nature. Moreover, I strive for a visual tension, either static or kinetic, to give each piece life.

When a prototype for a piece of furniture is finished, I look at it from all angles. Have I found the simplest, most perfect solution to my problem? Does the piece make a single, unified, visual statement? Does the piece work as a sculpture when viewed from any angle? Does each detail work by itself and, at the same time, add to, not detract from, the single statement of the piece? And, of course, is each strong and comfortable? Unless I can answer all of these in the affirmative, I go back to work.

Designers know that to find the simplest solution to a problem is a most difficult and time-consuming task. I hope you feel my work accomplishes this in a warm and charming way.

Bodyform chair. Peter J. Danko. 1982. Maple with black epoxy finish, wool, foam rubber. 30″ x 20½″ x 22″ (Danko Collection)

The Danko chair. Peter J. Danko. 1982. Poplar core with walnut veneer, leather upholstery. 30½″ x 21¾″ x 24″ (Museum of Fine Arts, Boston, purchased through funds provided by the National Endowment for the Arts, Ethan Allen, Inc., and the Robert Lehman Foundation)

John Dunnigan

West Kingston, Rhode Island

Born 1950

Educated at the Rhode Island School of Design
(MFA 1980), University of Rhode Island (BA
1971)

Selected Exhibitions: *Invitational 83*, The
Craftsman's Gallery, Scarsdale, New York,
1983; *Furniture Annual*, Elements, Greenwich,
Connecticut, 1983; *Post Modern Embellish-
ment*, Pritam & Eames, Easthampton, New
York, 1983; *New Handmade Furniture*,
American Craft Museum, New York, 1979

Artist's Statement:

Among the many requirements for a successful piece of furniture is that the
technology used should be appropriate to the purpose of the piece. In the
case of this console table, the techniques of steambending, laminating, and
veneering were necessary to achieve the desired effect. Yes, form does follow
this, that, the other thing, technology and function.

Console table and mirror. John Dunnigan. 1983. Padouk. 72″ x 36″ x 18″ (Dunnigan Collection)

William S. Hammersley

Richmond, Virginia

Born 1950

Educated at the University of Wisconsin (MFA 1976; BS 1972)

Selected Exhibitions: *Crafts Invitational,* Southeastern Center for the Arts, Winston-Salem, North Carolina, 1983; *Next Juried Show,* Virginia Museum of Fine Arts, Richmond, Virginia, 1983; *Five Decades,* Elvehjem Museum of Art, University of Wisconsin, Madison, 1981; *A Contribution to the Art of Living,* Cooper-Hewitt Museum, New York, 1981; *Young Americans,* Museum of Contemporary Crafts, New York, 1979

Artist's Statement:

I develop my work in the context of furniture in order to make use of the intimate nature of our relationship with objects we live with. Rather than taking a place in the tradition of styles of decorative design, I wish these works to have the promise of mystery, in the cause of their making, developed by our memories associated with saddles, boats, tools, odd boxes, etc., in order to connect with feelings we may have towards these things. I try to choose forms, images, and structures that fit the basic function but slightly alter the context. A chair and a saddle are both seating devices, so the saddle is placed in the context of a chair.

Utilizing the technique of bent lamination has been the easiest and most direct way to translate drawings into structures with wood.

Blue-Platform-1. William S. Hammersley. 1982. Red oak, dyed maple, brass. 41½″ x 54″ x 33″ (Hammersley Collection)

Thomas Hucker

Charlestown, Massachusetts

Born 1955

Educated at Boston University (Certificate of Mastery 1980), under Lenord Hilgner, Philadelphia, Pennsylvania (1974–76)

Selected Exhibitions: *New Handmade Furniture*, A.C.C. Exhibition, New York, 1979; *Young Americans*, Museum of Contemporary Crafts, New York, 1977

Artist's Statement:

Working with basic structure and proportion remains a major concern in my work. Each element must justify itself structurally as well as visually. The objects are nothing but the interaction of these elements as a cohesion.

This design system forces the natural properties of the material, and of external forces (i.e., the human body causing stress on the structure during use), to be more apparent and problematic. However, the way these issues are solved also constitutes the personality of the object, which can never be purely subjugated to these issues. In fact it is just the opposite, or the harmony of both that becomes rewarding.

Side chairs. Thomas Hucker. 1983. Walnut. 40″ x 23″ x 22″ (Hucker Collection)

Lawrence B. Hunter

Vista, California

Born 1931

Educated at University of California, Los Angeles (MA 1962), San Diego State (BA 1959)

Selected Exhibitions: *Second Annual Western States Invitational*, Gallery Faire, Mendocino, California, 1982; *Southern California Teacher/Craftsmen*, California State College, San Bernardino, California, 1981; *Fantasy Furniture*, Solo Exhibit, Boehm Gallery, Palomar College, California, 1980; *California Craftsmen*, Monterey Peninsula Museum of Art, Monterey, California, 1978

Artist's Statement:

I consider my furniture to be functional sculpture. Functional in that all the pieces have a use, and this use is carefully considered as part of the design. Sculpture because each piece is a statement, which I hope has significant form, which enriches the user through the visual senses as well as the functional uses. My clocks, for example, are kinetic sculptures which also tell time. They are designed to expose the workings of a time piece, making it a significant visual kinetic experience.

I use contemporary construction techniques, stack and bend laminations, grinders and other power tools. My goal is to be able to spend most of the time on the shaping of the piece, not on the construction. Whatever means possible I will use if it gives me the results that I desire. I am not a purist as far as construction, although when a shape needs to be shaped by hand, this I do; otherwise, I use power tools.

I believe furniture can enrich the life of the user, through its function and, more importantly, through the spirit or vitality I try to incorporate in the piece. Furniture has, through its function, a unique quality as an art form. Since one touches, feels, etc., the object as well as sees it, therefore a greater sense relationship occurs than is usually the case for pure sculpture where visual is the primary means of communication.

Clock V-2. Lawrence B. Hunter. 1983. Walnut, birch, brass, lead. 7' x 6' x 8' (Hunter Collection)

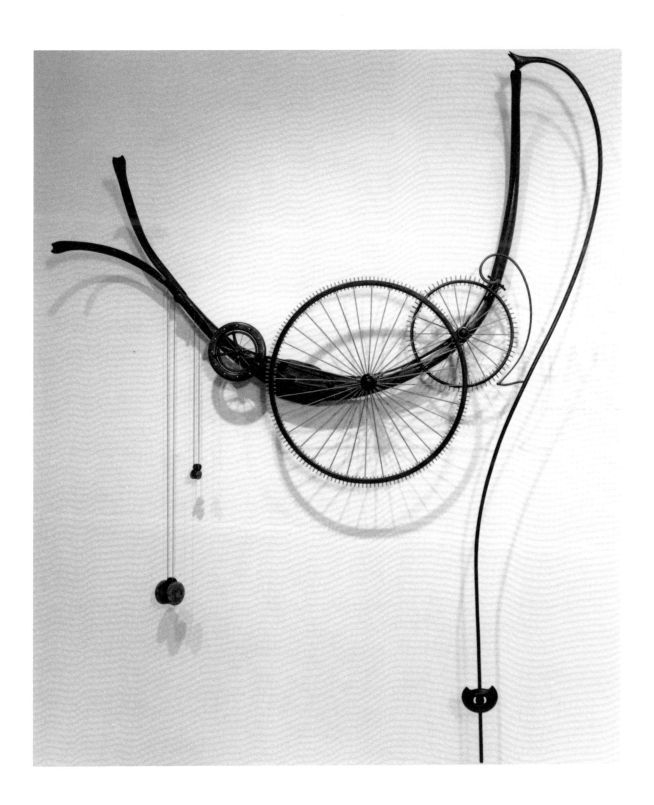

Dakota Jackson

New York, New York

Born 1949

Educated at City College of New York,
(BA 1971)

Selected Exhibitions: *Model Citizens Against Post Modernism*, sponsored by *Express* and The International Network for Art and Architecture, New York, 1982; *Further Furniture*, Multiples/Marian Goodman Gallery, New York, 1981; Group Show, Magnusson-Lee Gallery, Boston, Massachusetts, 1981

Artist's Statement:

As a native New Yorker, I have been designing and manufacturing furniture since 1969. As a professional magician into my early twenties, the transition to furniture making developed initially through the design and building of stage illusions. Indeed, my early furniture always included – as a signature – sophisticated hidden compartments.

Chair from "Jazz Collection." Dakota Jackson. 1983. Bent lacquered wood frame, anodized aluminum rods, leather seating. 32″ x 32″ x 30″ (Jackson Collection)

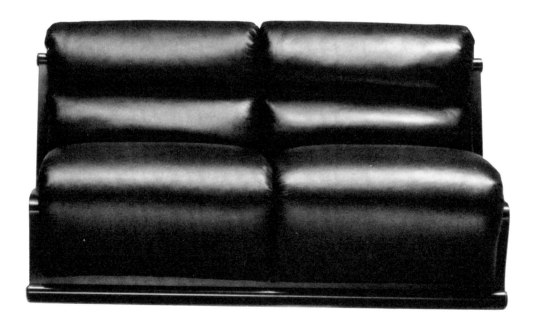

William Keyser

Honeoye Falls, New York

Born 1936

Educated at Rochester Institute of Technology (MFA 1961), Carnegie-Mellon University (BS 1958)

Selected Exhibitions: *Tables: New Variations*, Richard Kagan Gallery, Philadelphia, 1982; *Furniture from the Masters*, Pritam & Eames, Easthampton, New York, 1982; *New Handmade Furniture*, Museum of Contemporary Crafts, New York, 1979; *Contemporary Work by Master Craftsmen*, Museum of Fine Arts, Boston, 1977

Artist's Statement:

I'm interested in creating a composition of elements that appears to be haphazard and spontaneous, but which, upon closer inspection, reveals a logical and structural correctness.

This table is a random arrangement of arches, dancing along under the horizontal plane, at times venturing out to catch a glimpse above.

Low table. William Keyser. 1982. Pecan. 16″ x 16″ x 60″ (Mrs. Bernard Weinstein Collection)

Alphonse Mattia

Boston, Massachusetts

Born 1947

Educated at Rhode Island School of Design
(MFA 1973), Philadelphia College of Art (BFA,
1973)

Selected Exhibitions: *The Fine Art of the
Private Commission*, Dimock Gallery, George
Washington University, Washington, D.C.,
1982; *Art in the Home*, Portnoy-Goodman-
Jordan Volpe Gallery, Amagansett, New York,
1982; *A Case for Boxes*, Museum of Art, Rhode
Island School of Design, Providence, 1980;
Contemporary Works by Master Craftsmen,
Museum of Fine Arts, Boston, 1977

Artist's Statement:

I think that contemporary furniture, while playing with our feelings and
memories, should expand and redefine our notions about objects.

My approach to designing is essentiallly a problem-solving one. I work through
an elaborate sketching procedure before going to the full-scale drawings. The
sketch here is of several "bent-wood valets," a series that I am working on
presently that provides a format for simple form studies. With these valets I
am interested in combining practicality with humor, and hope to imbue the
pieces with a certain animated quality that relates to their function.

Valet. Alphonse Mattia. 1983. Ebonized walnut, assorted exotic hardwoods, polychromed ply,
metal and leather. 66″ x 18″ x 12″ (Mattia Collection)

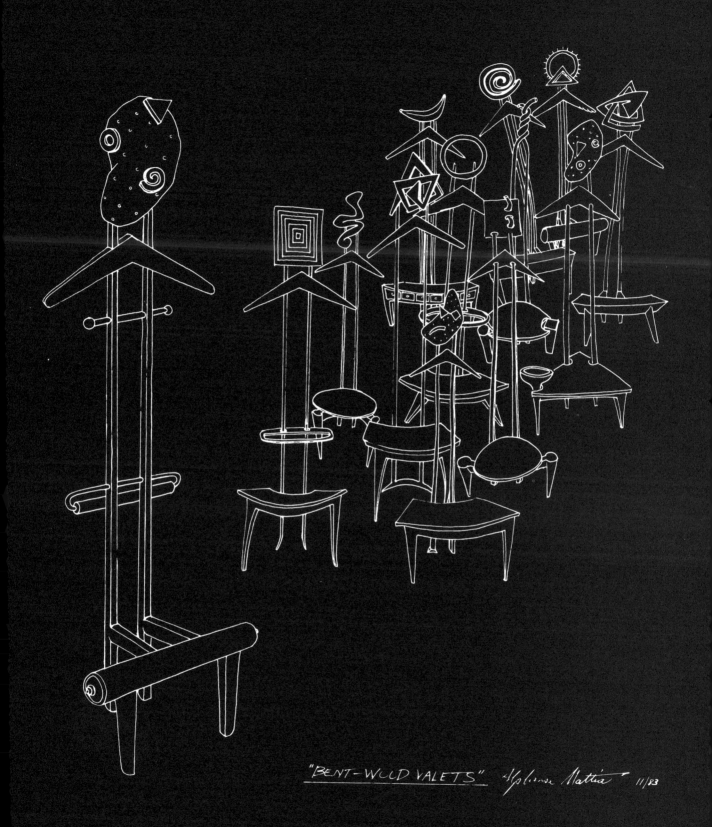

"BENT-WOOD VALETS" *Alphonse Mattia* 11/83

Jere Osgood

Wilton, New Hampshire

Born 1936

Educated at the Scandinavian Seminar of Denmark (1960–61), the School for American Craftsmen, Rochester Institute of Technology (BFA 1960), University of Illinois (1955–57)

Selected Exhibitions: *Studio Craft Furniture at Work*, Pritam & Eames, Easthampton, New York, 1983; *Tables, New Variations*, Kagan Gallery, Philadelphia, 1982; *New Handmade Furniture*, Museum of Contemporary Crafts, New York, 1979; Works of Master Craftsmen, Museum of Fine Arts, Boston, 1977

Artist's Statement:

You must use discretion when designing for bent lamination. Consider the overall design appearance first and have the technique evolve from it. Once you master the basic techniques, it is all too easy to conceive of a piece that could be executed in theory, but that in practice would be simply too hard to handle. Such a piece would probably be disorienting as well, so busy that one couldn't bear to be in the same room with it. I have found it best to stay with one design experiment in one piece of furniture, and to keep the rest of the piece restrained. Being able to build a piece of furniture that bulges wildly in all directions at once is not a good enough reason for doing so.

Chest of drawers. Jere Osgood. 1984. Andaman padouk. 20″ x 30″ x 56″ (Osgood Collection)

PERSPECTIVE SKETCH OF CHEST OF DRAWERS

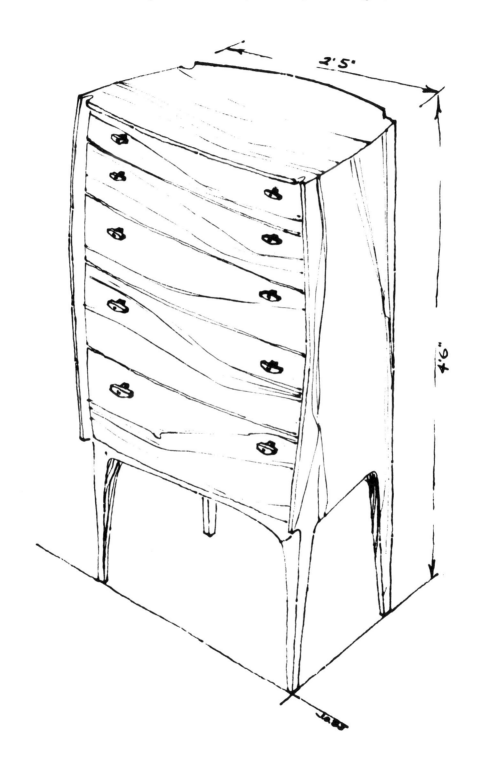

2'5"

4'6"

JB89

Martha Lynn Rising

Agoura, California

Born 1954

Educated at California State University, Northridge (MFA 1981, BA 1976)

Selected Exhibitions: *Wood Works*, Contemporary Images, Sherman Oaks, California, 1983; *Martha Rising: Wood*, Del Mano Gallery, Brentwood, California, 1982; *Furniture by Artists*, The Mandell Gallery, Los Angeles, 1981; *California Woodworkers*, The Oakland Museum of Art, Oakland, 1980

Artist's Statement:

My work has been likened to "sketches in the air" – a pencil moving through space leaving the form it traces solidly behind it. It is just this kind of freedom, ease, and motion that I try to portray. The motion of life and nature, which we all experience, has a vitality which, when portrayed, strikes a chord common to all. The dynamic vitality and rhythm I seek to give each piece allows a relationship to the piece beyond its utilitarian function – it portrays a moment of motion captured or portrayed in the piece. This common vocabulary of expression allows a communication beyond simply using or viewing the piece; I can express not only the way I experience life's energy and motion, but reflect the rhythms within me as I draw and design each work.

By building on the techniques which work best for me, developing forms and concepts which are most pleasing, I continually discover new possibilities and delights. The dynamic expression of flowing lines led first to bent lamination, then to curved joinery, adding joined and shaped graphic patterns of colorful woods, and on to the bending of these flowing patterns. Each process offers new challenges and possibilities for expression, forcing me on.

Of the challenges I set in my work, the greatest is working within the vocabulary of furniture and utilitarian function. I am an artist and I am a craftsman. My pieces are always intended to have a utilitarian as well as expressive, sculptural function. Working within the realm of function in utilitarian aspects creates incredibly challenging difficulties; however, I feel I gain a different kind of communication. I speak to people who see a chair and immediately realize they are seeing and experiencing much more. The objects we encounter daily are those with which we are most intimate. To carry some of that intimacy and understanding over to a piece that is at once also "art" or "sculpture" (the stuff set apart for museums, collectors, and galleries) perhaps touches new chords of understanding. My work is intended to touch and communicate, and seeking to find in each piece an integrity of expression, form, and function is in essence my goal and my delight in each piece I do.

Delight, Martha Lynn Rising. 1980. Maple, Andaman padouk, purpleheard, 33″ x 23″ x 48″ (Rising Collection)

Seth Lawrence Stem

Marblehead, Massachusetts

Born 1947

Educated at Virginia Commonwealth
University (MFA 1980), San Diego State
University (MFA 1977–78), Pennsylvania
State University (BA 1970)

Selected Exhibitions: *Interiors II*, Society of
Arts and Crafts, Boston, 1983; *RISD Leader-
ship in Crafts*, Craftsman's Gallery, Scarsdale,
New York, 1983; Furniture *Invitational*, Clark
Gallery, Lincoln, Massachusetts, 1983;
Woodforms, Brockton Art Museum, Brockton,
Massachusetts, 1981

Artist's Statement:

This cabinet is part of a series which explores the formal composition of several
controlled forms opposed by free form compound linear elements. I explore
the elaboration of function in my work, in the sense of exemplifying an ordinary
functional component in a visually flamboyant and physically extravagant
manner, as in the cabinet latch in this piece.

Jewelry cabinet. Seth Stem. 1983. Indian rosewood, cherry. 42″ x 23″ x 11½″ (Stem Collection)

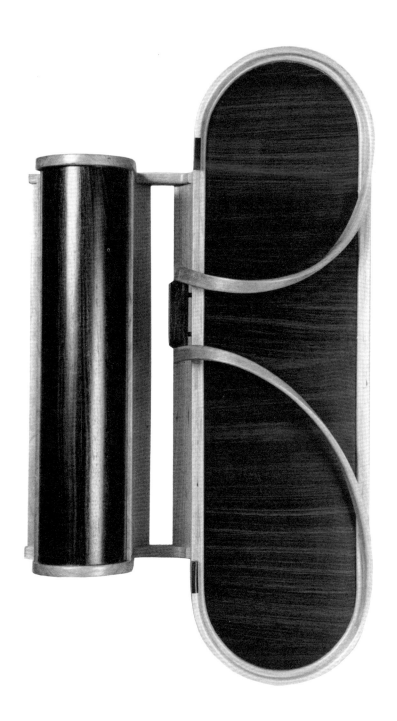

Photographic Credits

Unless otherwise noted all photographs are provided by the artists.

Gary Gilbert: cover, 14, 47
Royal Prince of Liechtenstein: 12
Gebrüder Thonet: 11, 13, 15
Thonet, Inc.: 1
Robert Thornton: 7, 8, 9, 10
Virginia Museum of Fine Arts: 31